LESSONS

WITH THE HUDSON GREATS

T0055819

Lessons:
BREAKING THE CODE
David Garibaldi

MODERN DRUMMER FESTIVAL 2008

GUEST APPEARANCE BY CARMINE APPICE'S SLAMM!

BILL STEWART

SIMON PHILLIPS

NDUGU CHANCLER

WILL CALHOUN

KEITH CARLOCK
THE BIG

JOHN BLACKWELL

HUDSON MUSIC MASTER SERIES

JASON BITTNER

WHAT DRIVES THE

A WORKBOOK FOR DRUMMERS OF ALL STYLES

HUDSON MUSIC®

LESSONS WITH THE HUDSON GREATS VOL. 1

Edited by Joe Bergamini

Book layout and design by Rick Gratton

Executive Producer: Rob Wallis
Original DVDs produced by Rob Wallis and Paul Siegel

Transcriptions and engraving by Willie Rose, except:
David Garibaldi transcriptions and engraving by David Garibaldi
Jason Bittner transcriptions by Jason Bittner and Willie Rose

DVD design, assembly, and authoring by Alfonse Giordano

All photos by Andrew Lepley except
Modern Drummer Festival 2008 photos by Christopher Otazo

Modern Drummer Festival™ is produced by Modern Drummer® Publications Inc.
Used by permission.
www.moderndrummer.com

All text written by Joe Bergamini

Table of Contents

Lessons with the Hudson Greats
Introduction

For quite a few years now, we at Hudson Music have been trying to add new features and interactivity to increase the educational value of our products for drummers. We have always tried to publish the most informative and useful products, but in recent years, we have tried to integrate audio and video with a view towards the new digital world. Our books always include audio, usually with play-along tracks, and now often including video. For our DVDs, this means that all of our major releases in recent years from Hudson have come with extensive eBooks on them. These eBooks are saved in PDF format in a separate folder on each DVD, and include detailed transcriptions and explanatory text that goes with the program presented on screen in the DVD. When watching the DVD, PDF icons appear on the screen, showing the example number to refer to in the eBook. By using the video and the PDF in tandem, you can almost create the environment of a private lesson, watching a specific example, and then studying the notation and immediately applying it in the practice room.

What has been interesting is that while we have received a lot of great feedback about these eBooks, and we are all constantly bombarded with news about the supremacy of the new all-digital world (and we ourselves now have apps such as Drum Guru that are on the cutting edge), we have found that many of our users have not made use of the PDFs to the full extent of their effectiveness. Perhaps it is because certain drummers are not very computer-savvy, or perhaps the extra step of having to place the DVD in their computer to access the PDF is inconvenient. We here at Hudson began to feel that we had a whole series of these fantastic eBooks that most drummers had not seen, even if they owned some of the DVDs on which they first appeared. And certainly even our biggest fan probably doesn't own all our DVDs, and could probably gain a lot of inspiration from a taste of some of these other artists. It was with this thought in mind that we embarked on this project.

What you hold in your hands is essentially a compilation of most of the eBooks that have appeared on Hudson DVDs starting with 2008's *Master Series: Antonio Sanchez*. When you look at all of these eBooks together, the list of world-class artists that they represent is staggering, and the amount of challenging practice material here (in all styles) is almost like a college course in modern professional drumset playing. We hope that this book serves a few different purposes. It is a companion workbook to all of our DVDs, presenting the eBooks in an attractive new format that can reside in your library and be referred to whenever working with any of the DVDs. It is also an incredible stand-alone product that allows you a glimpse into the key concepts of all the amazing players contained herein. Because we wanted to make sure the product worked on its own, we have included a two-and-a-half hour DVD containing selected clips from the original DVDs. The media icon in the text will clearly show which clips are included, and the chapter list on the DVD is also a handy tool for accessing a specific clip for practice.

Finally, we hope that working from a book/DVD package such as this one might allow you to gain inspiration and knowledge about the work of some of the drummers that perhaps you currently don't know very much about. Maybe you are a big fan of David Garibaldi already, but haven't yet discovered Aaron Spears. This package can expand your awareness and abilities on the instrument in a big way.

Enjoy the book and DVD, and we encourage you to put the material to use in the practice room. As always, we love to hear feedback from drummers all over the world, so feel free to visit www.hudsonmusic.com and let us know your thoughts.

Joe Bergamini
April 2013

eBook Intros

Jason Bittner:

The material in this chapter is taken from Jason's DVD *What Drives the Beat*. Jason presents a complete approach to developing the skills needed for metal drumming, including extensive material to build up your double bass drumming skills. He also presents a useful and interesting warm-up routine, which is applicable to all styles. The "Double Bass Crash Course" is a coordination routine that will develop the skills of all rock drummers, and in the "Metalfy" section, Jason shows how he allows ideas from other styles to morph into grooves that could be used in metal. On the DVD, you can see Jason explain all of these exercises in a clear and concise manner.

John Blackwell:

This eBook originally appeared on the Hudson Music DVD *Master Series: John Blackwell*. The DVD contains tons of the amazing playing that John has become known for. The transcriptions included here come from John's original compositions, as well as grooves from Justin Timberlake, Cameo, and others. Known for his amazing foot technique, here John brings out his former teacher Marcus Williams, who provides specially-designed exercises to develop fast foot technique. On the original DVD you can see John and Marcus trade drum licks.

Keith Carlock:

Keith is one of the most influential drummers of today. Here, in excerpts from his DVD *The Big Picture*, we see transcriptions of some of the sophisticated concepts that Keith puts to use to create his unique style. Keith emphasizes the importance of thinking and phrases, and many of the examples contained here show the advanced way in which Keith creates phrases, whether by using ghost notes, playing fills that extend over the bar line, or using other advanced timekeeping techniques. Also included in this section are some classic transcriptions of grooves that Keith played with Steely Dan.

David Garibaldi:

This chapter contains material from David Garibaldi's *Lessons: Breaking the Code* DVD. In the filming of that DVD, David explained and demonstrated concepts that appear in two of his books: *The Code of Funk* and *Future Sounds*. Much of this material resolves around two of David's signature concepts: the two-sound-level concept and the use of odd phrasing. The two-sound-level concept is a conceptual approach to playing that involves playing two basic dynamics on the kit: the ghost note and the main note. The interaction between these notes creates the funk sound. David's use of odd phrasing is represented here using his classic concepts of permutation and odd-numbered groupings.

Modern Drummer Festival 2008:

The examples in this section are taken from interviews which were filmed backstage at the Modern Drummer® Festival 2008. Each artist discussed topics relevant to their performance at the festival, and the included examples cover almost every style of drumming. The 2008 lineup was an especially excellent one, featuring Thomas Pridgen, Billy Ward, Will Calhoun, Ndugu Chancler, Simon Phillips, Derek Roddy, Dafnis Prieto, Todd Sucherman, Gavin Harrison, and Bill Stewart. All of these artists present challenging and useful concepts. Of special interest is Dafnis Prieto's section on Latin drumming, where he demonstrates many exciting musical examples.

 This icon indicates an example that is included on the accompanying DVD. Refer to the DVD chapter list to locate the clip.

Jason

WHAT **DRIVES** THE BEAT

Bittner

FORMING THE FOUNDATION PART 1: TWO-STEP BEAT

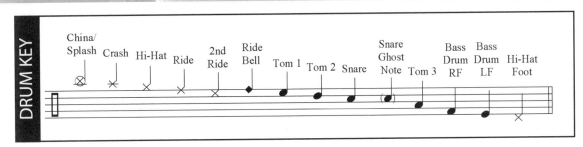

This section introduces two of the most important beats that form the foundation of modern metal drumming. On Jason's DVD, *What Drives the Beat*, all these examples are demonstrated. Jason recommends practicing all of these exercises with a metronome.

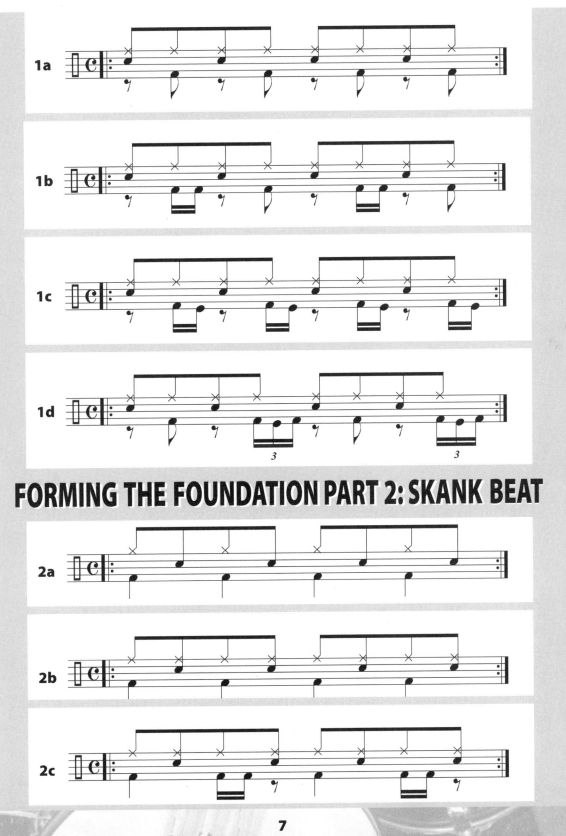

FORMING THE FOUNDATION PART 2: SKANK BEAT

JASON BITTNER

WHAT EVENS THE FEET

This section is designed to help develop equal strength and facility between the feet. Notice the right and left footings.

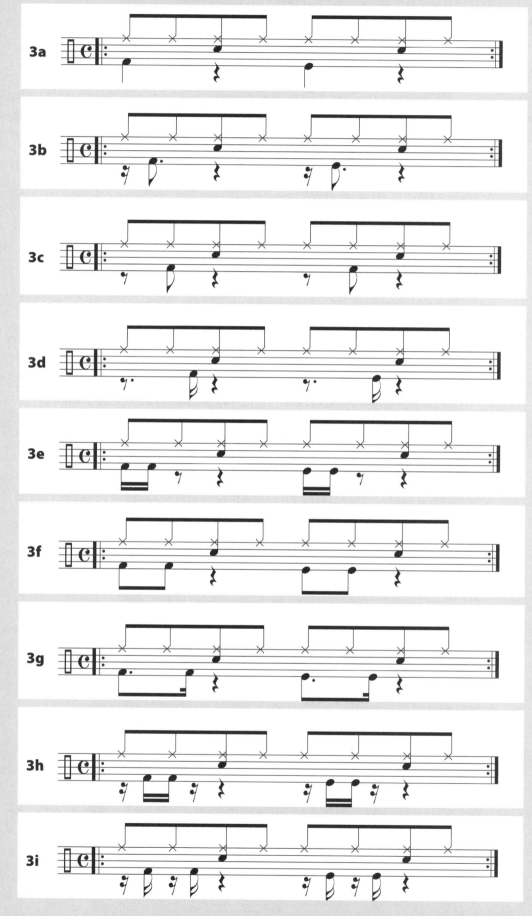

3j

3k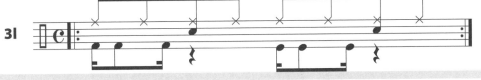

3l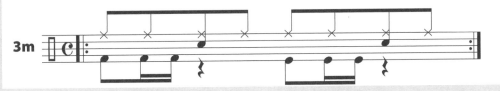

3m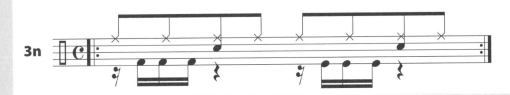

3n

3o

DOUBLE-BASS CRASH COURSE

This section presents a set of building blocks to develop a complete double-bass vocabulary. First, play these foot patterns:

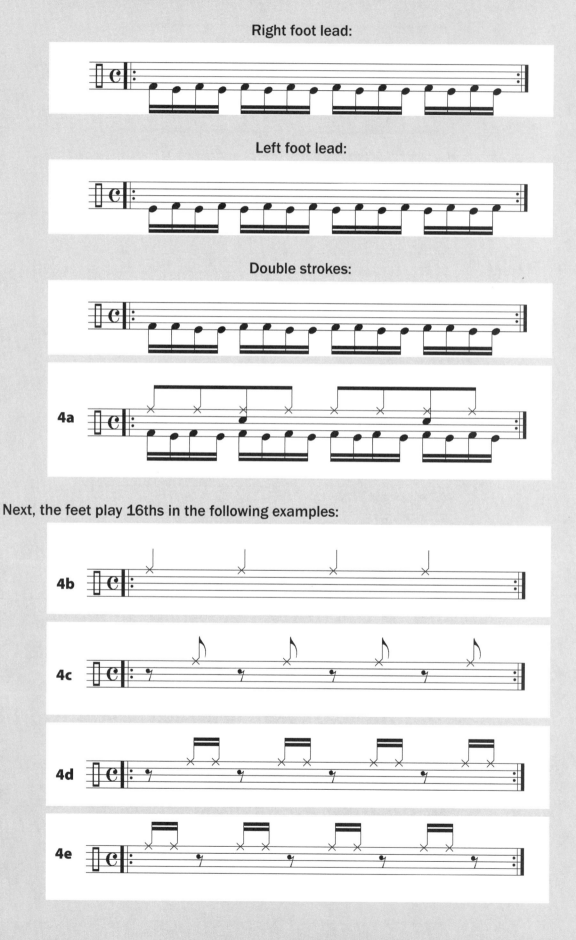

Right foot lead:

Left foot lead:

Double strokes:

Next, the feet play 16ths in the following examples:

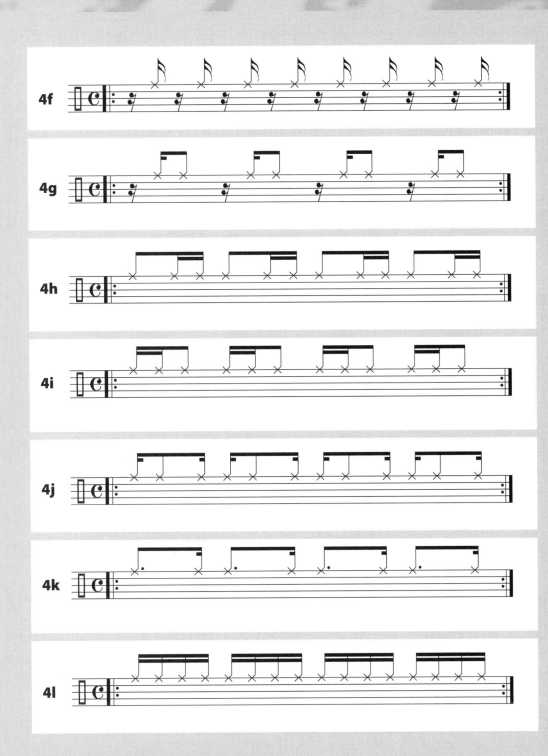

Then move to the following mixed rhythms:

Right foot lead:

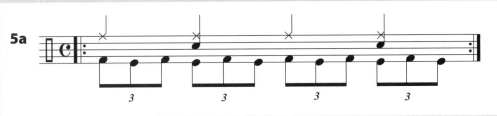

Left foot lead:

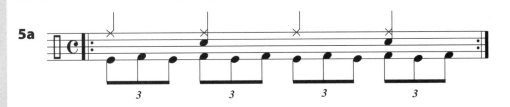

9

10

SHUFFLE PATTERNS

11

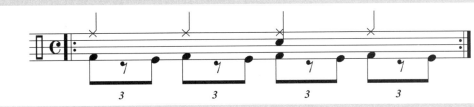

11a

11b

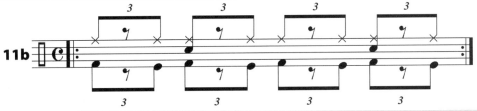

11c

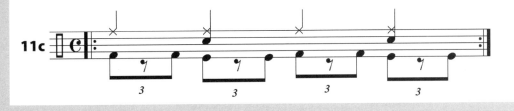

JASON BITTNER

COMBINATION PATTERNS

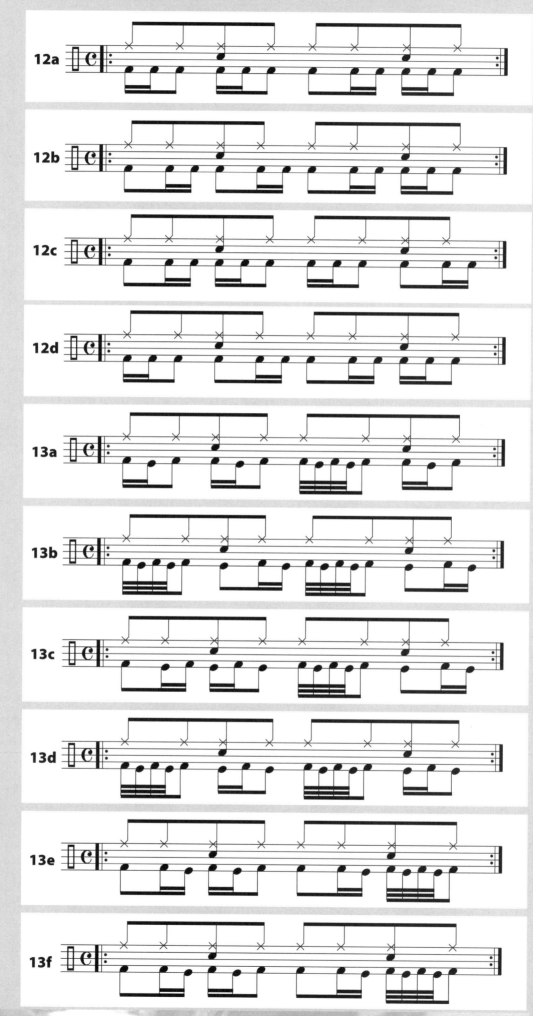

RUFFS

SHIFTING GEARS

These exercises will develop your ability to switch between different rhythmic pulses with the feet. Remember to practice with a metronome.

GALLOP EXERCISE

The gallop is a concept that Jason utilizes as a variation at fast tempos.

INTRO TO BLAST BEATS

Here are some blast beats that Jason uses. For more on this topic, check out *The Evolution of Blast Beats* book/CD by Derek Roddy (Hudson Ltd.).

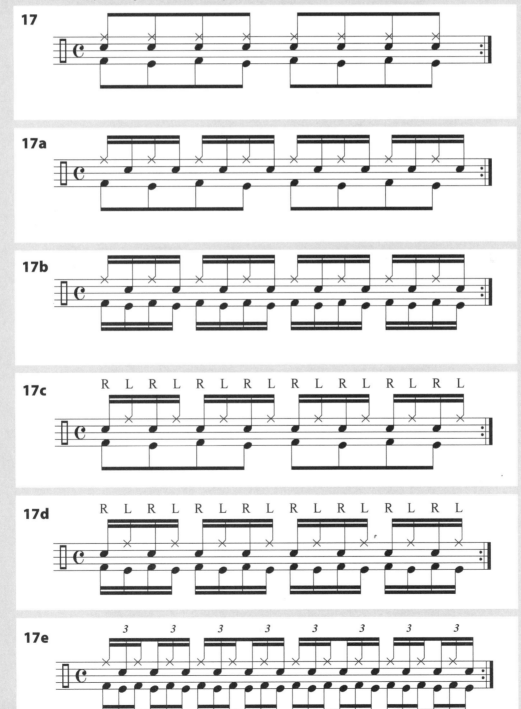

FILLS

FILL APPLICATIONS

Taken from "Destroyer of Senses":

Call and response fill based on 19a:

Taken from "Stillness":

"Power of I and I," "The Will to Rebuild," "Dread Uprising":

Taken from "Going, Going, Gone":

JACKHAMMER FILLS

The jackhammer fill concept involves playing the hands and feet in unison.

20C is taken from "Threads of Life."

LINEAR FILLS

"Linear" means only one limb hits at a time.

Quads:

Sixes:

THRASH/PUNK STYLE FILLS

Jason demonstrates these fills in the style of Dave Lombardo from Slayer.

TWO-HANDED RIDING

One of Jason's signature concepts is his use of two rides.

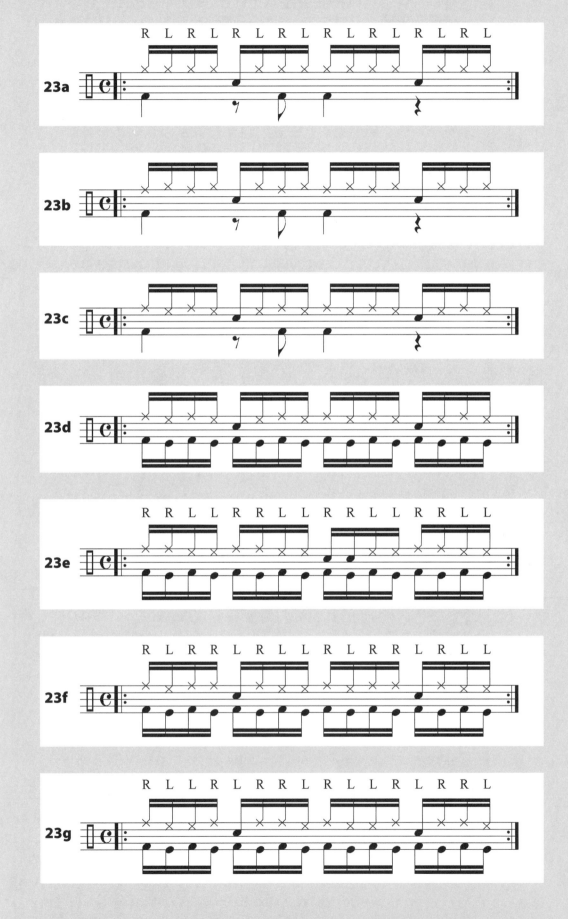

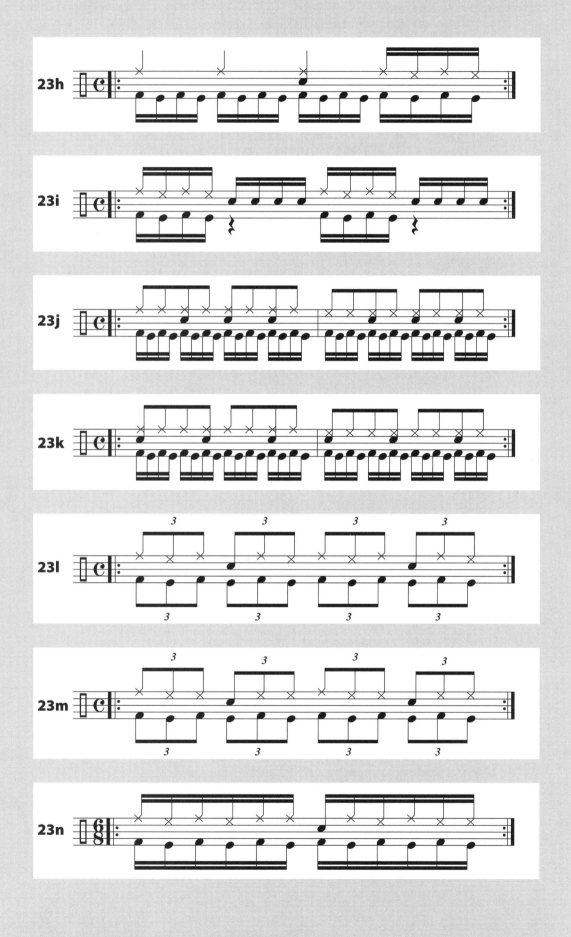

METALFY

The idea behind this section is to take non-rock stylistic concepts and apply them in a metal style, or "metalfy" them. First, Jason demonstrates a groove as it would be played in a given style, followed by the metalfied version.

JASON BITTNER

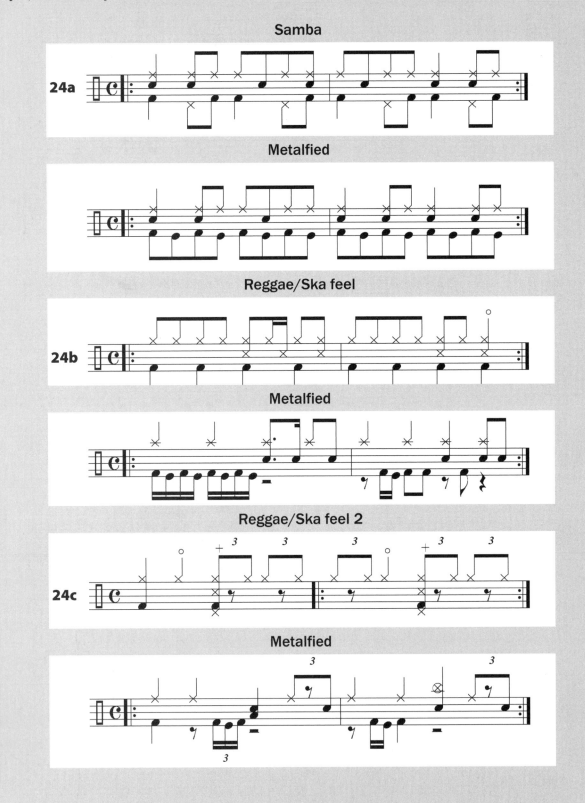

Country

Metalfied

Funk

Metalfied, used in the song "Stormwinds"

Nanigo

Metalfied, as used in "Gouging"

Slow Blues

24i

Metalfied

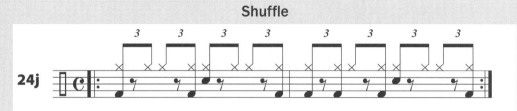

Shuffle

24j

Shuffle used in the song "Failure of the Devout"

24k

MASTER SERIES

John Blackwell

JOHN BLACKWELL
HUDSON MUSIC MASTER SERIES

"JEREMIAH'S SLEEPY NIGHT"

Here is the verse groove from John's song "Jeremiah's Sleepy Night."

"SEVEN YEARS OF GOOD LUCK"

Throughout the DVD, John demonstrates and discusses songs and grooves by his influences. Here is the groove from the Joe Sample song "Seven Years of Good Luck," originally played by drummer Omar Hakim.

"7-7-7-93-11"

This tune, recorded by The Time, featured this drum machine groove, demonstrated by John.

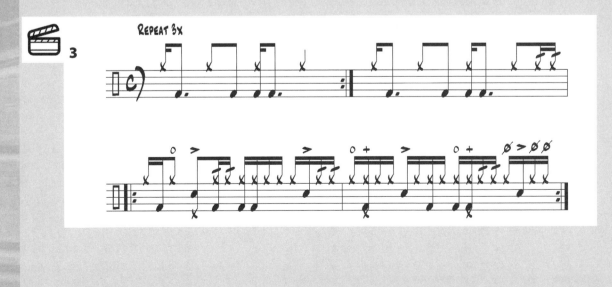

"LOVE STONE"

Here is a another example of John interpreting a drum machine groove, this time from a Justin Timberlake song.

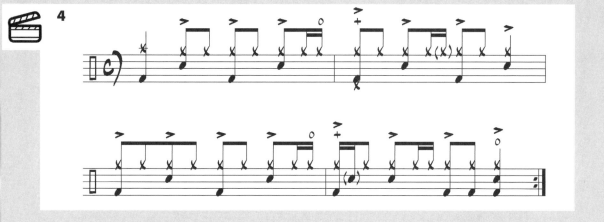

"FLIRT"

Here is a groove recorded by Larry Blackmon and Cameo. Cameo was a big influence on John. After many years of listening to their music, John was asked to play with the group.

"DO THAT STUFF"

John demonstrates a Parliament Funkadelic groove originally played by Jerome "Bigfoot" Brailey.

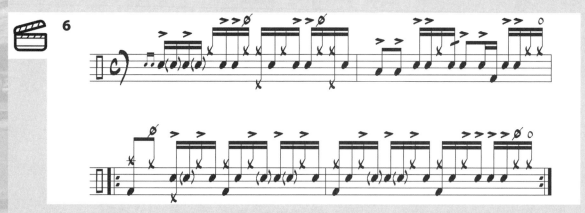

"MY LOVE"

John demonstrates the groove from another Justin Timberlake song.

MARCUS WILLIAMS EXAMPLES

Marcus first demonstrates a foot technique consisting of a ruff split between the bass drum and snare drum. Check out John's DVD for examples of Marcus playing this in context.

8

Marcus's next example is an exercise that can be used to build strength and speed. Marcus recommends playing his exercises on a very tight bass drum pedal.

9

Here Marcus demonstrates a lick consisting of five notes.

10a

When Marcus plays this lick in time, it looks like this:

10b

BILLY COBHAM-STYLE APPROACH

Here are two variations of Billy Cobham-style grooves demonstrated by John.

"WILD LIFE"

This groove, from the Tony Williams Lifetime album *Believe It,* influenced John while he was writing the song "Jada."

"JADA"

Here is the main groove from the song "Jada."

SLOW GROOVE EXAMPLE

John plays this groove to demonstrate the control and consistency necessary to play well at a slow tempo.

DENNIS CHAMBERS GROOVE

Dennis Chambers' playing with P-Funk was a big influence on John. Here he plays his interpretation of a groove he heard Dennis playing live with P-Funk.

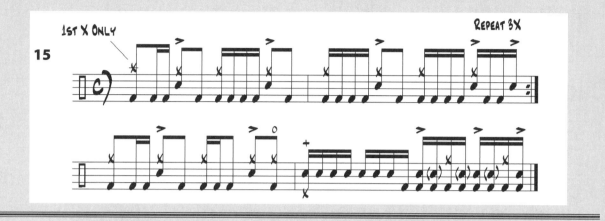

JOHN'S FOOT TECHNIQUE EXERCISES

John is often asked about his foot technique. On the DVD, he demonstrates the following Marcus Williams-style foot exercise:

Below is a transcription of John orchestrating the exercise.

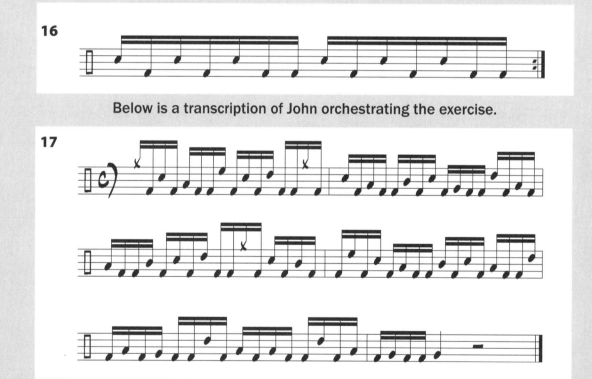

"MIND OF J"

John plays this groove during the verses of "Mind of J."

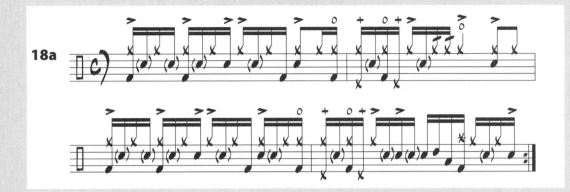

18a

Here is the instrumental vamp that John solos around at the end of the tune.

18b

In alphabetical order, here are some of the drummers mentioned on the DVD that have influenced John:

Carmine Appice, Larry Blackmon, John Blackwell Sr., Jerome "Bigfoot" Brailey, Gerry Brown, Dennis Chambers, Billy Cobham, Kenwood Dennard, Sheila E., Sonny Emory, Steve Gadd, Omar Hakim, Yogi Horton, Jonathan Moffett, Lenny Nelson, John Ramsay, Tony Thompson, Marcus Williams, Tony Williams

Keith Carlock

THE **BIG** PICTURE

KEITH CARLOCK
THE BIG PICTURE

PHRASING
IMPROVISATION
STYLE &
TECHNIQUE

HUDSON MUSIC

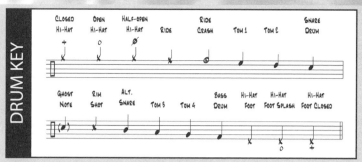

On *The Big Picture*, Keith demonstrates and explains many of the signature concepts that have made him one of the most copied drummers of today. Let's take a look at some of these concepts.

"Schizophrenic"

Here, Keith demonstrates the groove from this Oz Noy track.

Ghost-Note Levels Demo

This exercise is designed to demonstrate the difference in stroke height between Keith's ghost notes and accents.

Lining up the Bass Drum

When playing this exercise, be careful to make sure that the bass drum lines up exactly with the snare drum and hi-hat notes.

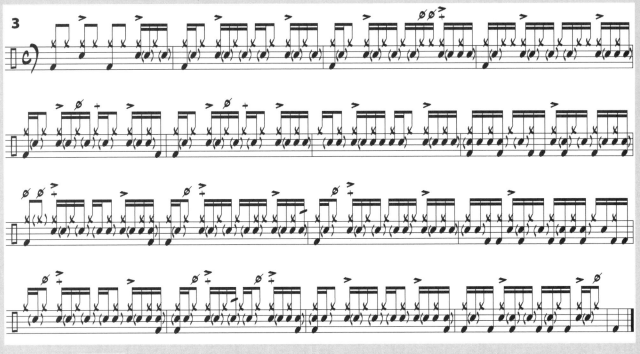

New Orleans-Influenced Grooves

Growing up in Mississippi, Keith was influenced by New Orleans music, and demonstrates the following groove examples on the DVD. Refer to the DVD to understand the slightly-swung feel of these grooves.

Groove Subdivision Demo

After playing the previous 2 examples, Keith plays this example at a slower tempo to emphasize the "in-the-cracks" (between straight and swung) feel of the groove.

New Orleans-Influenced Improvised Groove

Keith describes this as a Meters-influenced New Orleans-style groove idea.

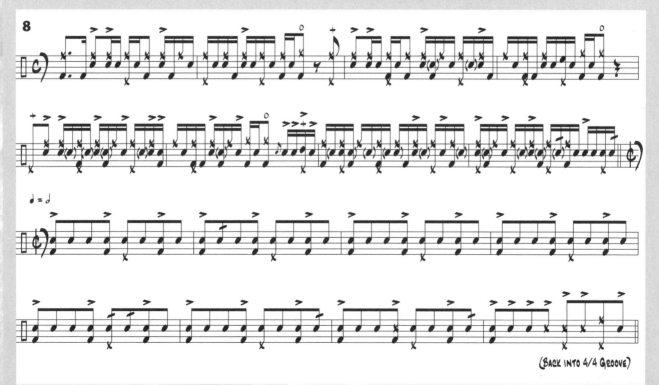

(BACK INTO 4/4 GROOVE)

Approach to Soloing/8-Bar Phrases

Whether playing a song or soloing, Keith is constantly thinking in 8-bar phrases. The following are soloistic examples that demonstrate this phrasing.

11

BACK INTO STRAIGHT TIME

🎬 4-Over-3 Groove Example

In the following groove, the ride cymbal, snare drum and bass drum are playing the 3 feel, while the left-foot hi-hat plays the 4 feel against it.

12

This alternate notation shows another way to think about this groove.

Incorporating the Hi-Hat Foot

The following examples show Keith demonstrating how he integrates the hi-hat in an improvisational way into his grooves. It can be thought of as the foot hi-hat replacing the bass drum in random places.

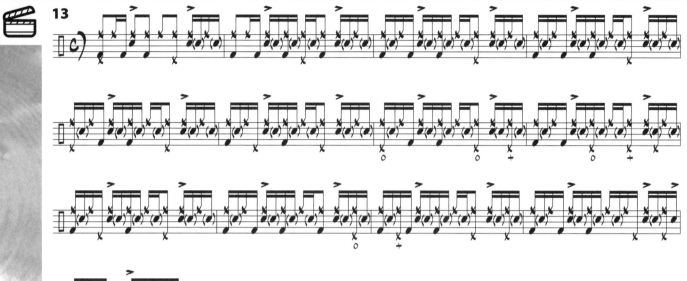

13

14

ETC.

Rudiment Applications

Examples 15 and 16 show different ways to apply 7-stroke rolls in your grooves.

Here is a 6-stroke roll application, beginning with a classic Motown fill.

Next are some flam applications.

19

"Lucky Beard"

The next two grooves are from the Wayne Krantz tune "Lucky Beard."

20

"Lucky Beard" 4/4 Bridge Groove

21

Overlapping Grace Notes

When playing the following exercise, focus on making sure the ghost notes on the snare drum do not flam with the notes on the bass drum.

22

Hand/Foot Combination

Here, Keith is playing rudimental figures between the snare drum and the bass drum.

"Jackass Surcharge" Main Groove

This groove is from another Wayne Krantz song.

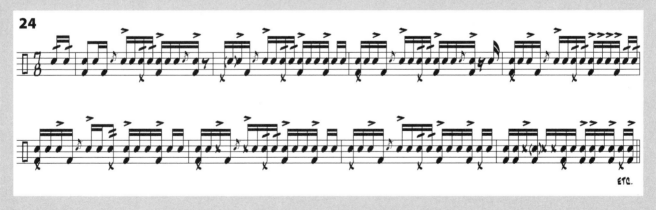

KEITH CARLOCK

"Ice Pick" Main Groove

The groove for this Oz Noy tune has a shuffle feel.

Steely Dan Grooves: "The Last Mall"

Keith was the drummer on the original recording of the next 3 songs.

"Godwhacker"

"Two Against Nature"

KEITH CARLOCK

Here are Keith's interpretations of some classic Steely Dan songs.

"The Fez"

This is Keith's interpretation of Bernard Purdie's classic groove from "The Fez."

"Kid Charlemagne"

This is another Bernard Purdie groove interpreted by Keith.

"Josie"

The original track featured Jim Keltner on drums.

Wayne Krantz Trio: "Riff"

Here is the main groove that Keith plays on this tune with the trio.

ETC.

KEITH CARLOCK

Fills:

The next 5 examples deal with Keith's approach to playing fills.

Fill Idea Demo

This idea shows Keith taking a sticking, breaking it up in different ways rhythmically, and orchestrating it around the kit in various ways.

6/8 Fill Demo

Keith demonstrates the following example with the trio, using the same basic sticking as above, but this time in 6/8.

R R L R R L L R R L L   R L R R L L R R L L   R L R R L L R R L L   R L R R L L R R L L   ETC.

6/8 Fill Demo Ending on 1

In this example, the phrasing is more simple, with the fill idea resolving on beat 1.

L L R L L   R L R L L

L L R L L   R L R L L

6/8 Fills with Click

Keith stresses the importance of practicing all of these concepts with a click, and demonstrates the following idea. The odd groupings in the second line are an example of an area where Keith plays a sticking idea that "floats" over the time.

4/4 Fills with Click

Warm-Up Exercises

Keith uses various rudimental stickings to warm up.

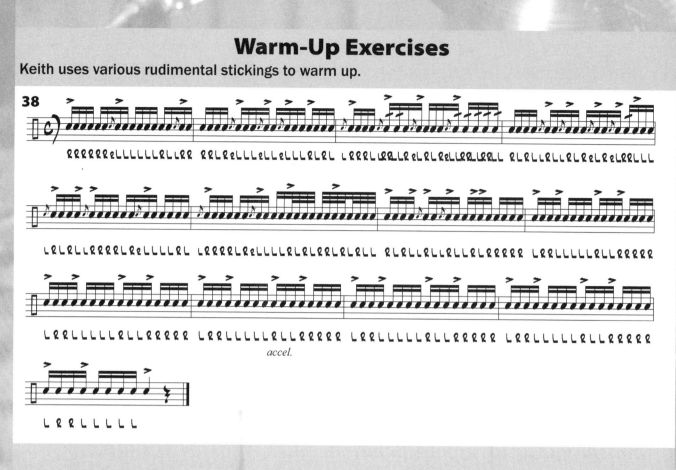

Finger Technique Exercises

On the DVD, Keith explains that the use of his fingers is a major component of his hand technique. He demonstrates the following example as a way to build facility with your finger strokes.

Foot Technique Groove Demo

Here, Keith demonstrates finger strokes applied to a groove.

Warm-Up Exercises

Here are more warm-up exercises. Keith uses rudiments and patterns he learned in drum corps/marching band when warming up.

Odd Phrasing Exercise

Keith stresses the importance of thinking in 8-bar phrases, however, in actual performance he does not state the beginning of each phrase so obviously. When practicing this, count so that you don't lose your place.

David

LESSONS
BREAKING THE CODE

Garibaldi

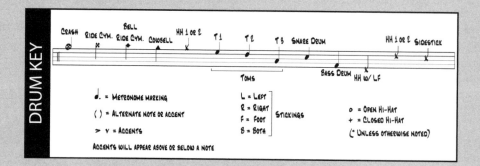

Check out David's *Lessons: Breaking the Code* DVD and *The Code of Funk* book/CD package to hear all the songs and examples that are not included in this package.

"PAGE ONE"
(J. Tamelier, S. Kupka, E. Castillo)

This piece is in the style of an earlier Tower of Power composition, "Soul Vaccination." "Soul Vaccination" was the first song we put together that was based on a non-traditional rhythmic structure... no 2 & 4 drum grooves! The success of this concept opened the floodgates for us, in that we were no longer limited to typical R&B beats as the rhythmic base for our material.

Tower of Power music is based in tradition, but also experimentation. Much of our music was inspired by the music of James Brown, Motown, Stax/Volt, etc., but also with a significant infusion of jazz and Latin music concepts. We use the R&B idea of rhythm section parts: everyone in the section has a role to play; a composed part that in a performance will have some improvisation. Adhering to a part gives the music structure and organization.

As far as the drum parts go, anything will work, at least in theory. I approach the music with this mindset, and then edit as we develop ideas. The concept for this piece was very wide open: my instruction was to "do your thing," but with very little, if any, 2 & 4 snare drum.

Ex. 1a is the main groove of the song: a long pattern (4 bars). The right hand plays the right hi-hat, and the left hand plays the snare drum and left hi-hat.

1a

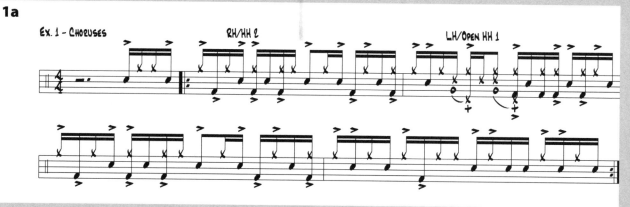

Ex. 1b is a shorter 2 bar pattern.

1b

Ex. 1c is the keyboard solo groove, which stays within the rhythmic framework established in the chorus and verse.

1c

Ex. 3 - Organ Solo

LF/HH - 8TH NOTES...RH/RC

Ex.1d is the ending section...here I use the 2 & 4 snare drum to release the tension created in the previous sections.

1d Ex. 4 - Choruses Out

LF/HH - 8TH NOTES

"POCKETFUL OF SOUL"

(S. Kupka, E. Castillo, H. Matthews)

The basic drumset concept for "Pocketful of Soul" was inspired by Afro-Cuban drumming. With my group Talking Drums, many of our compositions were in 6/8. There was no traditional drumset part to any of the rhythms we explored, so I had to invent my own parts. I put the grooves together in the same way I approached funk beats, the difference being triplets instead of sixteenth notes.

The results were ear-opening to say the least, and I saw the potential for some very creative groove-making. Rather than the obvious shuffle, I opted for a more syncopated approach—think Tower of Power meets James Brown ("Gonna Have A Funky Good Time") and Los Muñequitos.

The entire song is in 12/8: one dotted quarter note = one beat, or 4/4 using eighth-note triplets: three eighth notes to the quarter note, one quarter note = one beat. (Basically a shuffle, but playing all of the triplets.)

Listen to *The Code of Funk* DVD-ROM (or the *Lessons* DVD performance), which contains the original drum track and follow along with the transcription to get comfortable with how the song is counted. Once you're comfortable with that, then start putting the grooves together.

Here's what I played during the choruses on the recording:

2a Choruses - CD Version

Ex. 1

Here's what I play during the choruses on the live version:

2b Choruses - Live Version

Ex. 2

DAVID GARIBALDI

Once we started performing the song live, I expanded the basic groove to fit with the two-bar pattern the rhythm section was playing.

My drum set parts evolve as we perform the songs. Here is the 2004 live version of the horn soli:

RH/Bell, LH/SD, HH

There are many 6/8 ideas and coordination concepts in my other instructional books that could help in the understanding of how to put these kind of grooves together. Many of those beats could work in sections of this song.

"BACK IN THE DAY"
(Skip Mesquite, Steve Mesquite)

This composition revolves around 2 basic grooves, the verses:

Ex. 1

...and the choruses:

Ex. 2

...with the exception of the "twists and turns" of the arrangement, I stayed with these basic parts throughout out the song—a very simple approach with very little improvisation until the choruses at the end.

There is an ensemble figure at measure 81, which is an eighth note on the "&" of beat four. Staring with measure 89, this figure occurs every four measures, and is interpreted three ways:

Ex.3 – ...preceded, or set up, by a fill...

Ex.4 - ...part of the groove...(two variations)

Ex. 5 -

The concept here is to "suspend" the sound across the bar line, following the length of the figure, while keeping the momentum of the groove going forward. The initial figure (meas. 81) is played with crash cymbal and bass drum. After that (meas. 93 to end), either a snare drum with crash cymbal, or snare drum with open hi-hat.

Choruses 7 and 8 include all three interpretations:

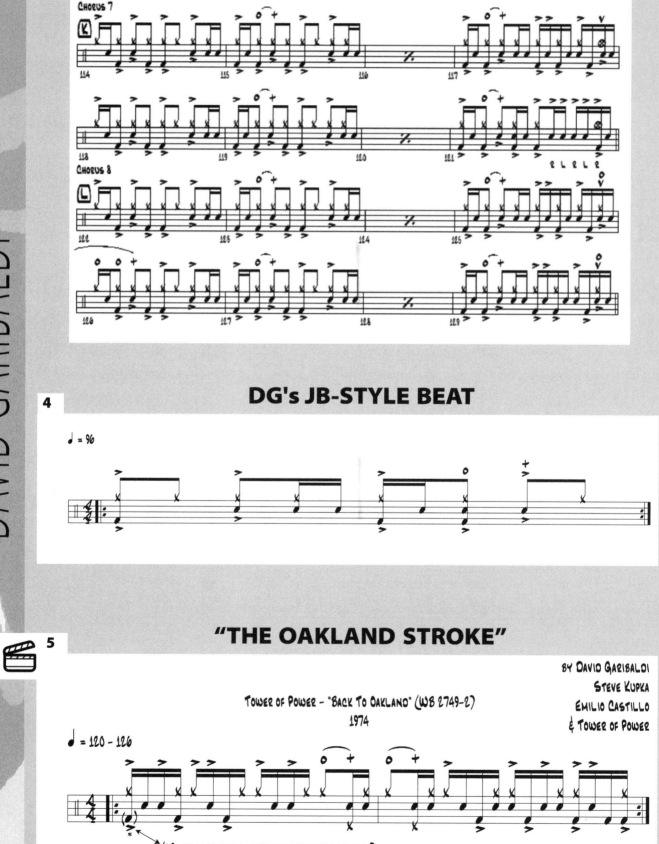

DG's JB-STYLE BEAT

"THE OAKLAND STROKE"

BY DAVID GARIBALDI
STEVE KUPKA
EMILIO CASTILLO
& TOWER OF POWER

TOWER OF POWER - "BACK TO OAKLAND" (WB 2749-2)
1974

(*OMIT BASS DRUM NOTE WHEN PATTERN REPEATS)

DAVID GARIBALDI

THE TWO-SOUND-LEVEL CONCEPT

This graph illustrates the dynamic relationships between the hi-hat, snare drum, and bass drum in David's playing:

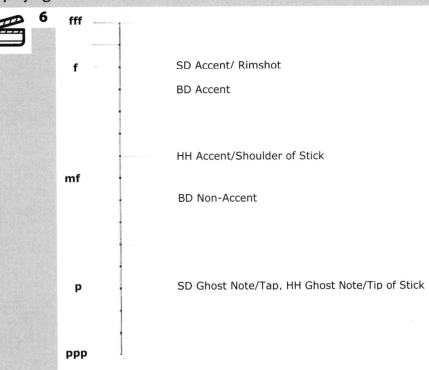

6

fff	
f	SD Accent/ Rimshot
	BD Accent
	HH Accent/Shoulder of Stick
mf	
	BD Non-Accent
p	SD Ghost Note/Tap, HH Ghost Note/Tip of Stick
ppp	

The dynamics of the music being played controls these levels. The following examples are played on the DVD to demonstrate this concept. The main objective of this exercise is to focus on acheiving the proper sound and texture of the snare drum ghosted notes. The secondary objective is to create a shaker-like weave between the hi-hat and snare drum ghosted notes. Start slowly to build control, then gradually increase the tempo while maintaining the sound.

6a

6b

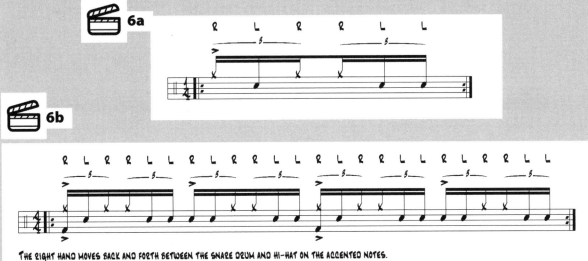

THE RIGHT HAND MOVES BACK AND FORTH BETWEEN THE SNARE DRUM AND HI-HAT ON THE ACCENTED NOTES.
THE LEFT HAND MAINTAINS THE LOW STICK HEIGHT ON THE SNARE DRUM.

6c

THE FOOT HI-HAT VOICE

This page expands on 6C and is bonus material not demonstrated on the DVD.

IN THE POCKET v3.1

DAVID GARIBALDI

This is a series of groove ideas that build new variations around a basic initial idea.

DAVID GARIBALDI

These examples are demonstrated on the *Lessons: Breaking the Code* DVD, to demonstrate David's concept of permutation: moving one or more notes throughout the bar.

THE BASIC PERMUTATION CONCEPT (One Voice)

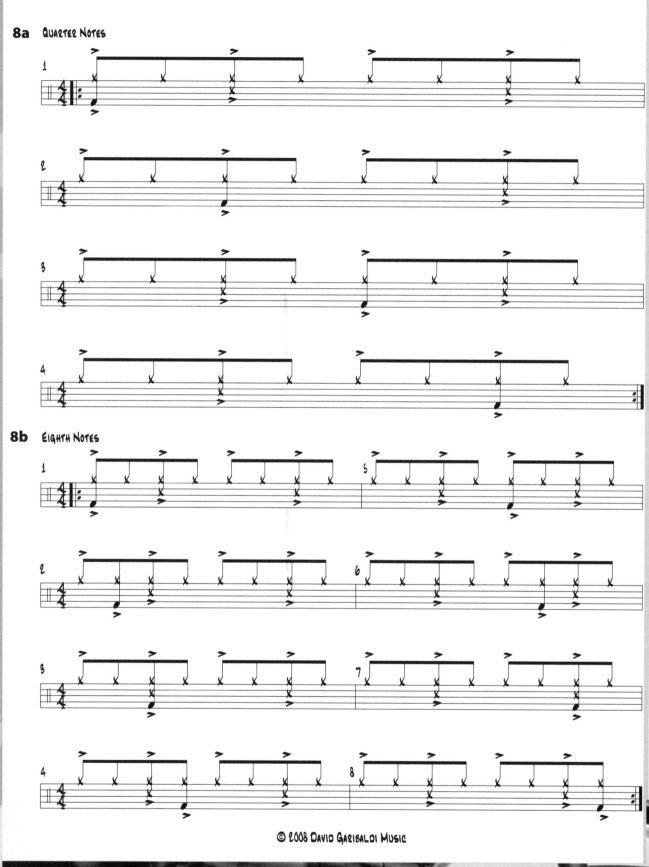

DAVID GARIBALDI

The Basic Permutation Concept (One Voice)...cont. — 2 —
Sixteenth Notes

APPLIED PERMUTATION

This section demonstrates how to apply the concept of permutation. For this section I use the basic groove from the song "Eastside." "Eastside" is based on a jam that the rhythm section performed on Rocco's *Bass Day 1998* DVD (Hudson Music). The basic one-measure groove is typical TOP: a mix of inspiration from the great drummers of the James Brown bands, combined with an idea I got from studying the concepts of Gary Chaffee. On my DVD, I demonstrate this groove along to the "Eastside" loop from *The Code of Funk*.

I then demonstrate how to permutate this groove in various ways. At the end of these demonstrations, I explain the concept of adding an open hi-hat note in various places to create the permutations. NOTE: This next example is not an exact transcription from the DVD, but comes from the recorded version of "Eastside." On the DVD, I play the same concepts, but not in this exact order. The DVD segment and the transcription below will allow you to see conceptually what is happening.

In this section I randomly add an additional quarter note to the end of the basic pattern. This allows the groove to go back and forth from 5/4 to 4/4. In Ex. 2, a 16-bar section, the odd and even measures are bracketed to delineate each time signature. The 3/4 measure at the end was needed so that I could land on the downbeat of the next chorus.

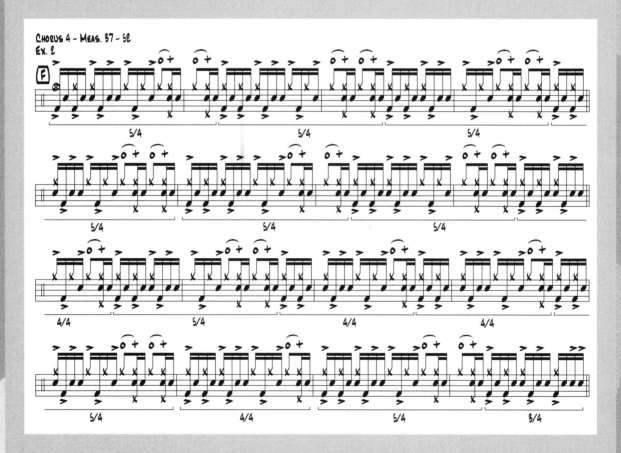

STRETCH THAT GROOVE! - Pt.1

Reprinted with permission of Modern Drummer magazine.

As I look back at all I've learned throughout my music life, probably the most useful tool I've found in building drumset technique and vocabulary has been the concept of permutation. This is how I develop the ability to hear unusual rhythms. I think of it as a Rhythmic Solfeggio System. Solfeggio is the concept used to train your ear to hear note intervals.

Permutation can be used to teach you to hear unusual rhythms as they relate to whatever time signature you may be in. I've covered this topic many, many times in my books, articles, and clinics. It's very simple, but incredibly elastic and adaptable; it works with every style, because it's not a style but is what I consider to be a root concept. You can learn this right along side the rudiments, and all technique building.

For those of you who are new to this, permutation is a mathematical concept, and can be defined as "all the possible ways to order a group of numbers." For example, take the numbers one through four. We can order those numbers in this way:

1 2 3 4...or...4 1 2 3...or...3 4 1 2...or...2 3 4 1

Rhythm is mathematical, so therefore the permutation concept can be applied to any rhythm or time signature.

The time signature we're using is 4/4: four beats to the measure, and a quarter note gets one beat. In Ex. 1-4, we've applied this permutation idea by permutating Ex.1 through quarter notes. Moving the last beat of the measure to the front of the measure, and then repeating that, gives us the variations. This is the permutation concept applied to a time signature.

Brackets are used beneath each exercise to further illustrate how this works. Take beat 4 from Ex.1, move it to the front of the measure, and this produces Ex.2, and so on.

This study is written for two hi-hats, positioned so you can perform in an open-handed way. The right hand plays one hi-hat (HH2), while the left hand plays the other hi-hat (HH1) and snare drum.

There are five groups of four exercises...twenty exercises total, all based on Ex.1-4, and all use this quarter note permutation idea. Each four-exercise group uses the same hand combination, but different foot combinations. All four limbs are used to create these time feels. Once you can perform Ex.1-4, the rest are basically the same, but with changes in the feet.

Go slowly, and make sure to count aloud while performing each exercise. Counting aloud—an often under-appreciated concept—will "ground" you and help to unify all your limbs, as you're hearing yourself speak. The results will surprise you.

Don't forget to pay attention to the sound levels as well: accurate accents, very quiet and delicate ghosted notes.

A detailed explanation of permutation and sound levels can be found in my book *Future Sounds*. If you're really brave, try playing some of these with the loops that are included in The *Code of Funk*.

DAVID GARIBALDI

STRETCH THAT GROOVE! - Pt.1

David Garibaldi

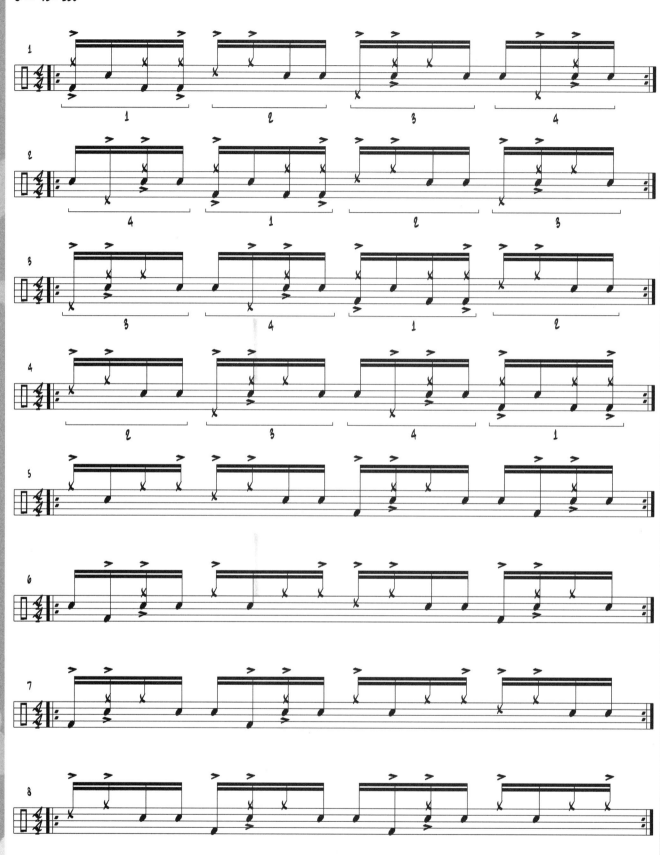

DAVID GARIBALDI

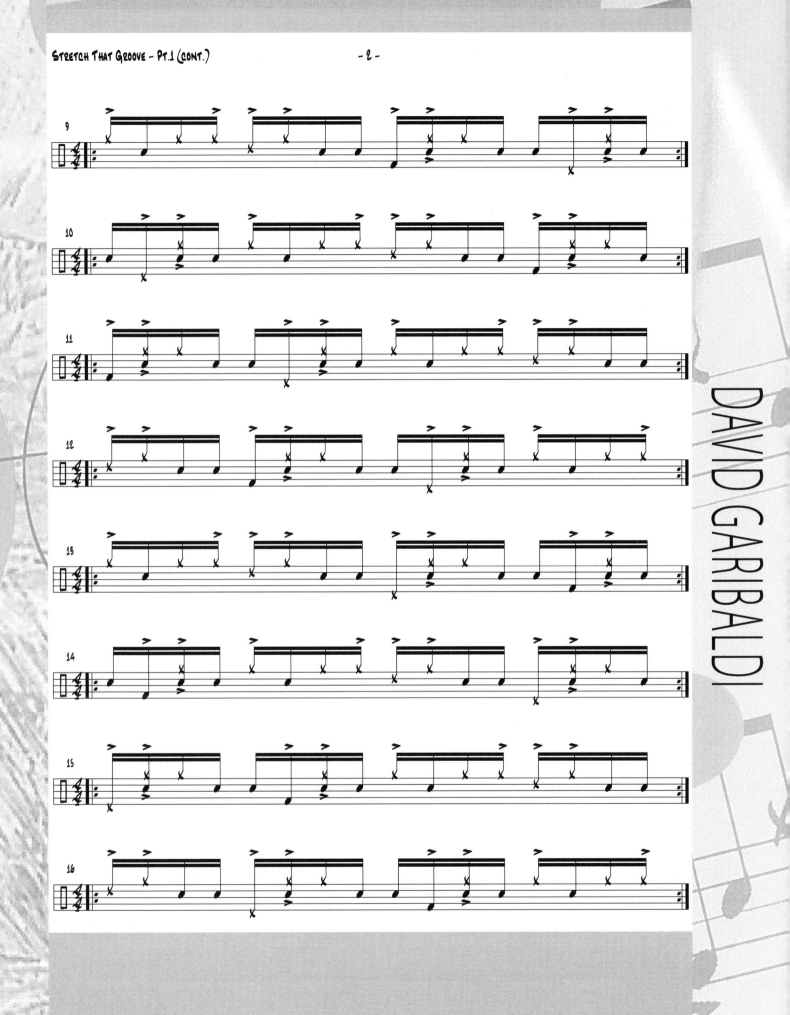

DAVID GARIBALDI

STRETCH THAT GROOVE! - Pt.2

Reprinted with permission of Modern Drummer magazine.

Last time, we looked a very powerful rhythmic concept called permutation, which can be used to teach you to hear unusual rhythms as they relate to whatever time signature you may be in. Here in part 2, we'll take additional steps to further develop the basic idea discussed in part 1.

First, let's look at where we began...as in part 1, we're using an open-handed approach, so you'll need an additional closed hi-hat positioned somewhere on the opposite side of the drum set.

This gives us four voices to work with: hi-hat 1, snare drum, bass drum, and hi-hat 2. Hi-hat 1 is played with the left hand and left foot, hi-hat 2 is played with the right hand.

Here is the basic groove (Ex. 1) from part 1:

Once there is an understanding of the content in part 1, which explains how to play and permutate this groove, the next steps involve first making a few changes. Looking at this 4/4 measure, the five-note phrase beginning on beat three, when repeated, adds two more notes, changing the time signature to 9/8.

Next, I've added the sticking, which I've found to be helpful when working out challenging coordination problems.

Here is where we begin in part 2. The goal of part 2 is to be able to play this 9/8 phrase within 4/4. We will develop this in three ways:

1. Play the 9/8 groove, as written, so as to be able to hear the flow of the entire phrase. I'm feeling this as 4 – 4 – 5 – 5. A right paradiddle (4), a left paradiddle (4), and two five-note phrases (5 – 5).

2. Play individual measures as grooves. Each individual measure can be learned as a separate event.

3. Connect these measures, one at a time, until you can play all nine as a cycle through 4/4 (9/8 within 4/4).

Exercises 1 – 9, in 4/4, contain nine 9/8 phrases. The brackets under each phrase show how they fall in relation to each 4/4 measure.

IMPORTANT KEY: Count all the sixteenth notes aloud.

Start slowly, with each individual 4/4 measure, counting aloud.

Connect each measure, one by one, counting aloud in 4/4, until the entire 9/8 phrase can be played within 4/4. The complete phrase, played within 4/4, takes nine measures of 4/4 to complete. This will take some time, because you're training your ear to hear one time signature while you play another. Eventually, your ear adjusts, and you'll be able to play any odd phrases you can think of, within 4/4.

Once you can do this, you'll most likely end up with many of your own ideas...this is what you want. Follow those ideas.

Don't let the challenge of these exercises intimidate you. When I started working on these kinds of ideas, I could do none of it. I only had an idea...a thought. I followed my instinct, and it took me to many other places I never would have gone, had I rejected the initial inspiration.

Finding your own voice begins with following these moments of insight, and here's where practice becomes your partner: you start working through your ideas, and then, over time, these ideas are shaped into workable concepts...concepts that reach into every corner of your musical life.

Make no mistake, practice is work, but practice = success. Be relentless in the pursuit of yourself, for your brain is capable of amazing things, and above all, have fun doing it!

DAVID GARIBALDI

DAVID GARIBALDI

STRETCH THAT GROOVE! - Pt.2

♩ = 92 - 110

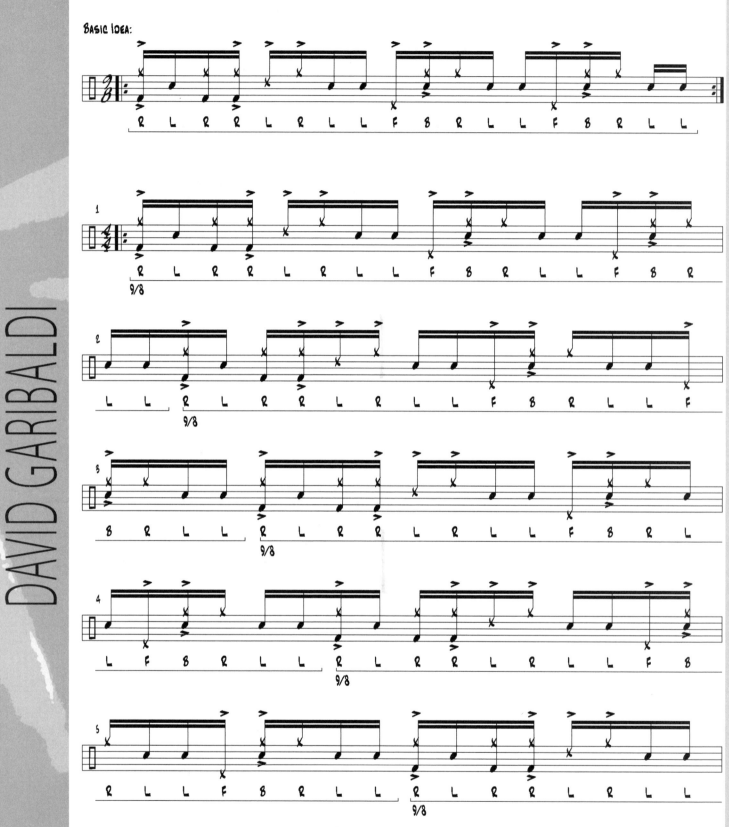

12

♩ = 88-106

The next series of examples shows several odd-numbered sticking combinations that David uses in a funky way.

FIVE-A-DIDDLES

DAVID GARIBALDI

13

SEVEN-A-DIDDLES

DAVID GARIBALDI

NINE-A-DIDDLES v.1

♩ = 88 - 106

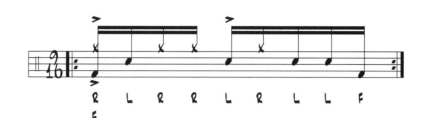

R L R R L R L L F
R
F

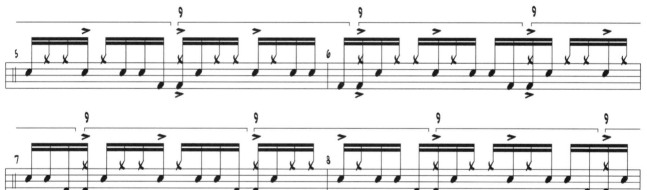

DAVID GARIBALDI

NINE-A-DIDDLES v.2

David Garibaldi

ELEVEN-A-DIDDLES

David Garibaldi

♩ = 88 - 106

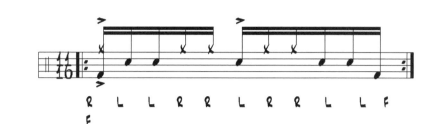

R L L R R L R R L L F
F

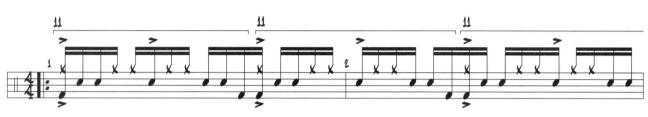

David Garibaldi

MARTIAN THIRTEENZ

David Garibaldi

Modern Drummer

INTERVIEWS

MODERN DRUMMER® FESTIVAL™ 2008

TODD SUCHERMAN

THOMAS PRIDGEN

BILL STEWART

GUEST APPEARANCE BY CARMINE APPICE'S SLAMM!

DAFNIS PRIETO

DEREK RODDY

SIMON PHILLIPS

NDUGU CHANCLER

BILLY WARD

GAVIN HARRISON

WILL CALHOUN

eBook included

HUDSON MUSIC

Festival

2008

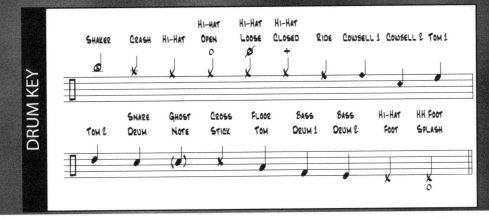

The examples included here from the 2008 Modern Drummer Festival were discussed and demonstrated during the backstage interview segments on the *Modern Drummer Festival 2008* DVD.

Thomas Pridgen

Moving Doubles

Thomas uses these exercises to help develop single-foot double strokes on the bass drum.

Thomas demonstrates this technique in the following solo:

Getting Around The Kit

Thomas uses these exercises to help develop speed around the kit.

Open-Handed Playing

Thomas plays the following grooves leading with both right and left hands.

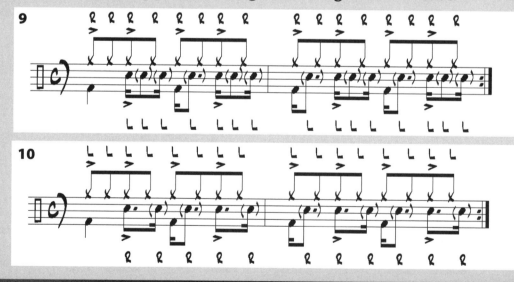

Billy Ward

Billy Ward
Groove Concepts

In the following grooves, Billy uses a shaker in his right hand, playing it in the air and also striking the hi-hat with it.

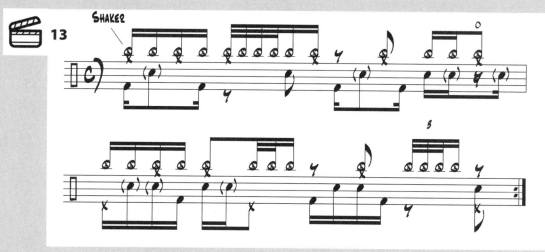

Billy utilizes hi-hat openings to add variation to his grooves.

Here is an example demonstrated by Billy in the style of Bernard Purdie:

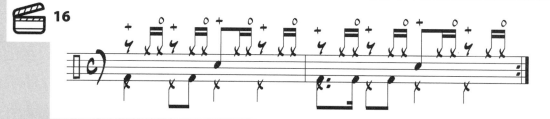

The following grooves utilize the shaker once again. In exercise 17, watch out for the 3-over-2 polyrhythm.

18

Exercise 19 is an example of a 12/8 blues groove.

19

Billy discusses hearing the following subdivisions ("gears") while playing a 12/8 groove.

20

Jazz Triplets

Exercises 21-25 are a series of variations for triplets in a jazz context.

21

22

23

24

25

Robbie Robertson: "Hold Back the Dawn"

Billy plays the following basic grooves on the Robbie Robertson song "Hold Back the Dawn."

26

27

Will Calhoun
African-Inspired Concepts

Will demonstrates these Nigerian-based interpretations of a James Brown-style groove:

28

29

This example shows a traditional Nigerian interpretation of an ensemble figure.

30

Example 31 demonstrates a funk/James Brown-style interpretation of the same figure.

31

Will demonstrates several examples of traditional African 6/8 patterns and variations.

32

Ndugu Chancler

Adding Accents

Groove demonstrating basic accent sound:

Miles Davis: "Directions"

Ndugu demonstrates the basic groove he played on the Miles Davis tune "Directions."

Ndugu demonstrates the following groove as a variation to add more motion/drive to the main "Directions" groove.

Simon Phillips
Snare Drum Warm-Up

Simon demonstrates the following warm-up during his interview. The idea here is to make sure the sound between the hands is absolutely even.

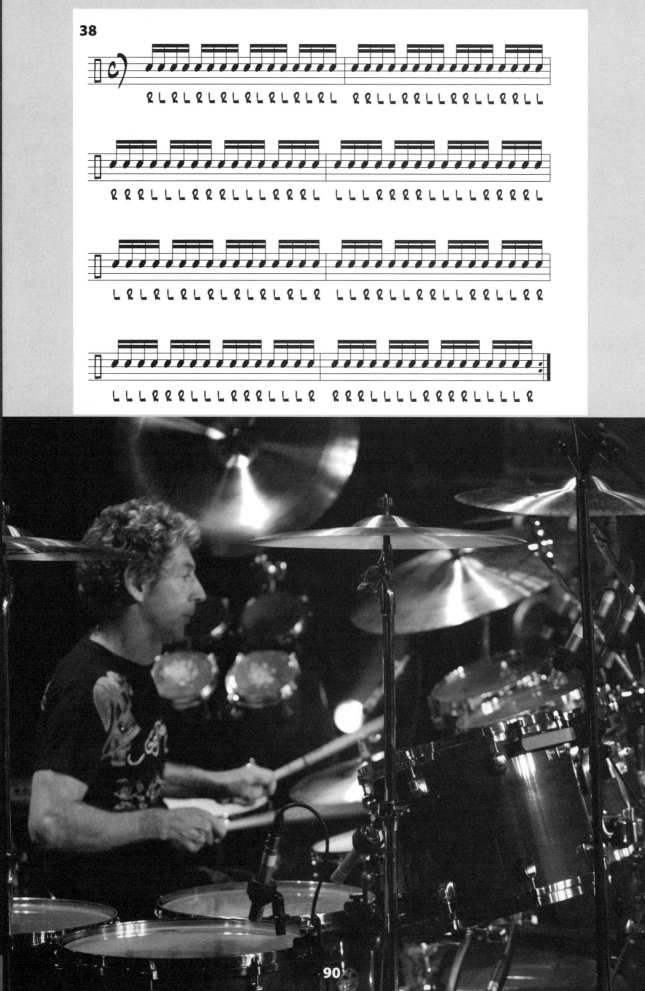

Derek Roddy

Refer to Derek's DVD, *Blast Beats Evolved,* and his book/CD package, *The Evolution of Blast Beats,* for an incredibly complete approach the high technical and stylistic demands of extreme metal. Derek also has a fun DVD for all levels that addresses setting up and getting comfortable with your kit, entitled *Playing with Your Drums.*

Blast Beats and Other Concepts

Exercise 39 is an example of a blast beat split between the feet.

Exercise 40 is a blast beat split between the floor tom and bass drum.

In Exercise 41, Derek demonstrates how to comp a guitar line with his hi-hat foot:

Exercise 42 will help you build left foot strength.

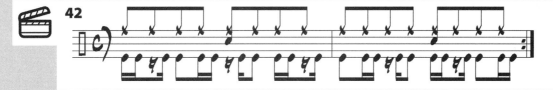

The following two exercises will help improve your balance while playing double bass patterns.

Dafnis Prieto
Afro-Cuban Grooves

Dafnis demonstrates various Afro-Cuban concepts during his interview. The first example is a demonstration of rhumba.

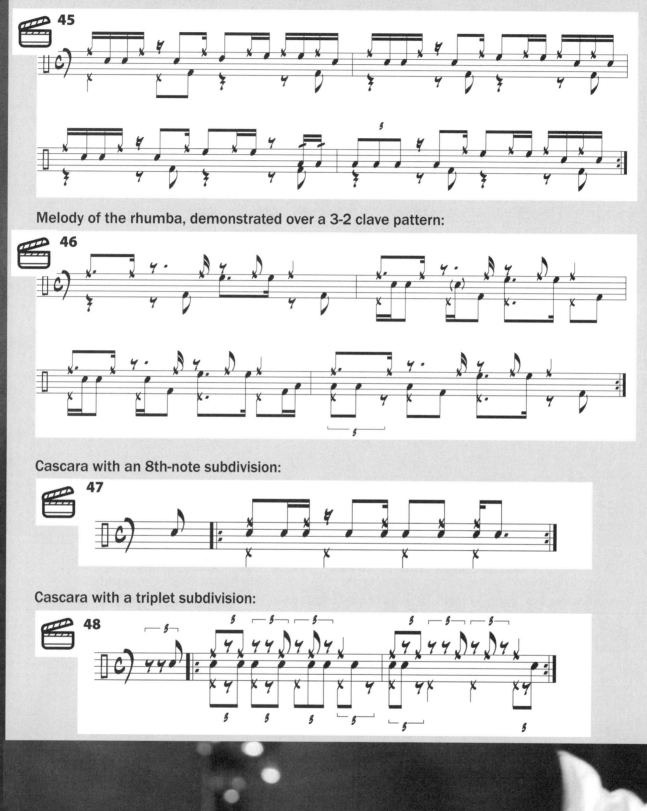

Melody of the rhumba, demonstrated over a 3-2 clave pattern:

Cascara with an 8th-note subdivision:

Cascara with a triplet subdivision:

In this example, Dafnis plays straight 8th notes while accenting the cascara. He then fills in the off-beat 16ths with his bass drum.

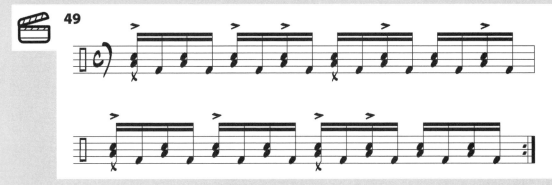

Here are some cascara variations on the bells.

Exercise 51 demonstrates how Dafnis executes the transition between Afro-Cuban and swing feels in a Latin jazz context.

Dafnis feels 6/8 in a 4 pulse, as shown in this groove:

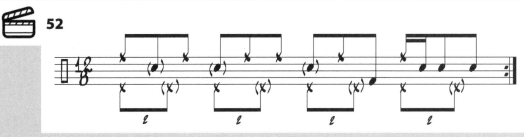

Abakwa groove:

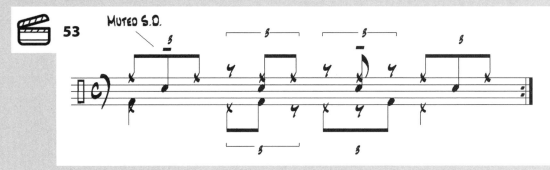

Songo groove:

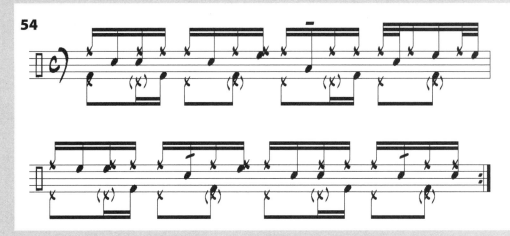

Danzon, a traditional Cuban dance. The clave is played for reference purposes only.

Todd Sucherman

These are just brief excerpts from Todd's interview, but a full method and approach to his playing can be found on his DVDs, *Methods and Mechanics I & II*, and detailed transcriptions with play-along tracks can be found in his book/CD package, the *Methods and Mechanics* companion book.

Flam Patterns

Todd demonstrates the following flam patterns:

56

57

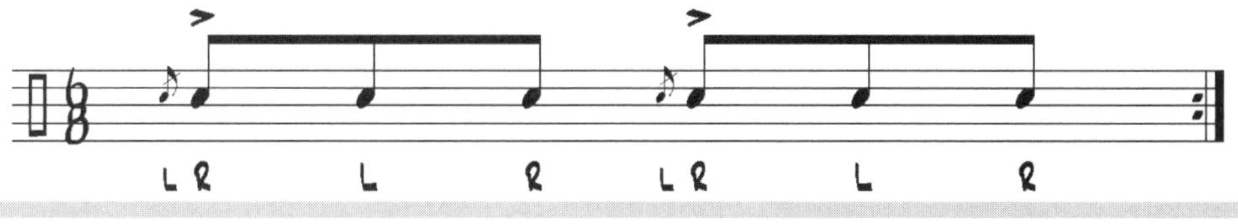

58

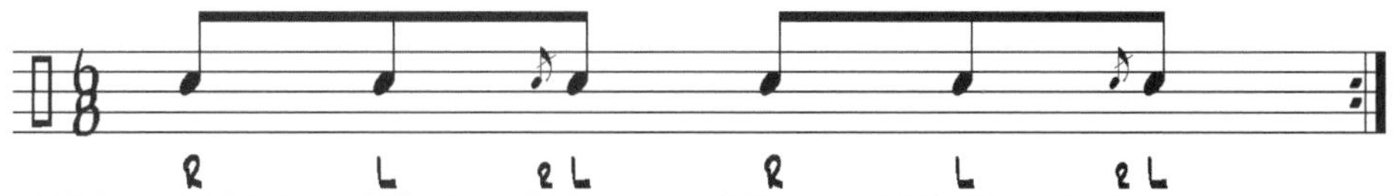

The following exercises apply flams to the drumset.

59

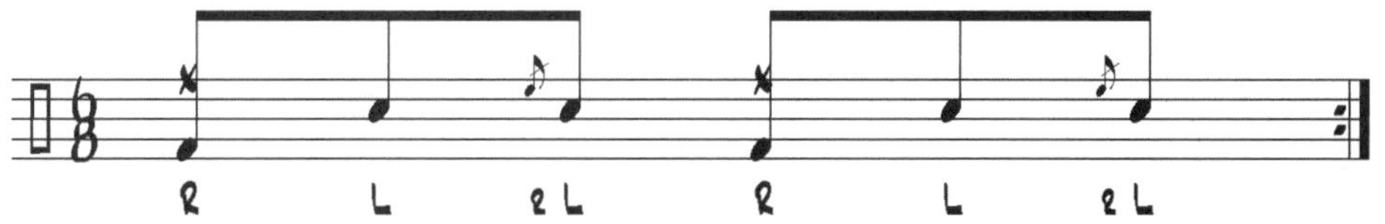

60

Polyrhythmic Paradiddle Pattern

Exercise 61 is a 4-over-3 paradiddle lick demonstrated by Todd:

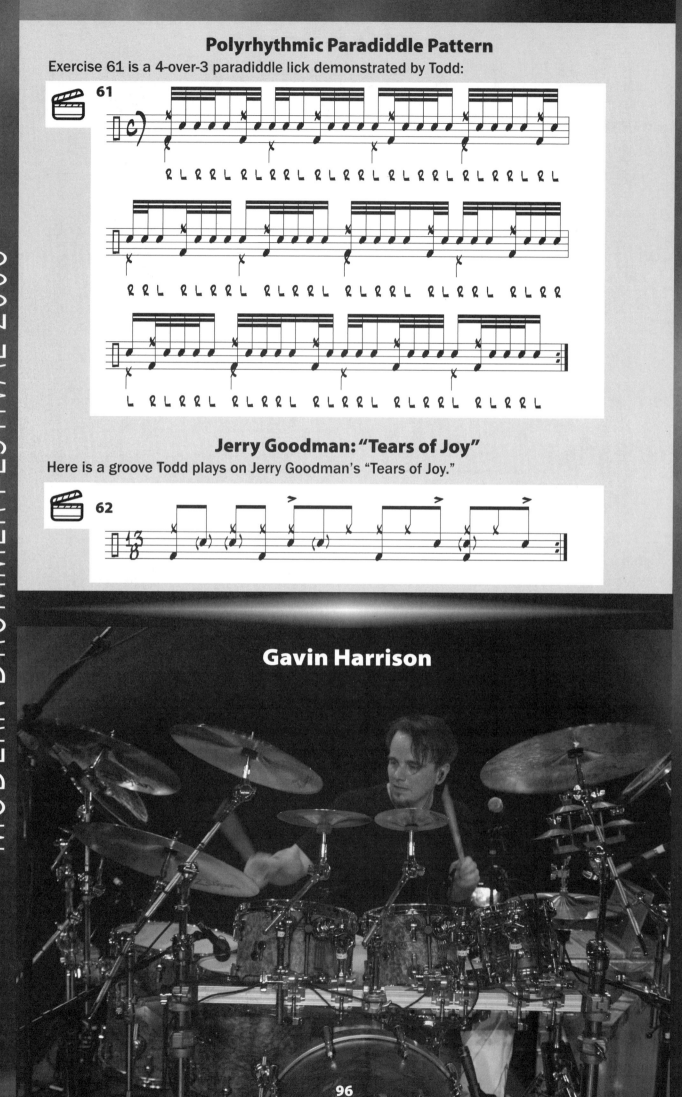

Jerry Goodman: "Tears of Joy"

Here is a groove Todd plays on Jerry Goodman's "Tears of Joy."

Gavin Harrison

Gavin Harrison

Gavin has a complete line of books and DVDs available that detail his approach to progressive concepts such as beat displacement and polyrhythmic drumming, including his *Rhythmic Visions* and *Rhythmic Horizons* DVDs, and *Rhythmic Designs* book/DVD package, all available from Hudson Music.

Overriding

In the following examples, Gavin demonstrates his concept of overriding. First is a simple groove in 7/8.

In exercise 64, Gavin accents every other eighth note to create a quarter-note pulse that crosses over the barline.

Exercise 65 is an example of a choppy way to play in 7/8.

By only playing quarter notes, Gavin smoothes out the groove and gives listeners something solid to lock into.

In Exercise 67, Gavin takes it one step further by only accenting every third sixteenth note.

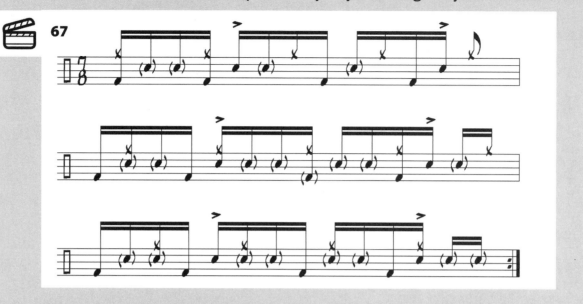

Bill Stewart

Swing Timekeeping Concepts

In Exercise 68, Bill demonstrates a simple way to keep time in a jazz setting.

Exercise 69 demonstrates ways to embellish the ride pattern.

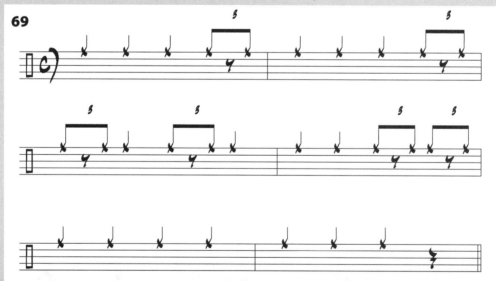

Here are two variations of the feel of the ride pattern. Exercise 70 is more open, while Exercise 71 has a tighter feel:

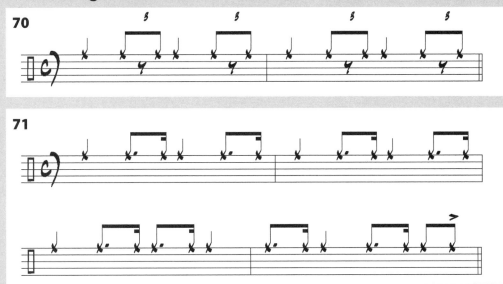

Here are some variations for uptempo ride patterns:

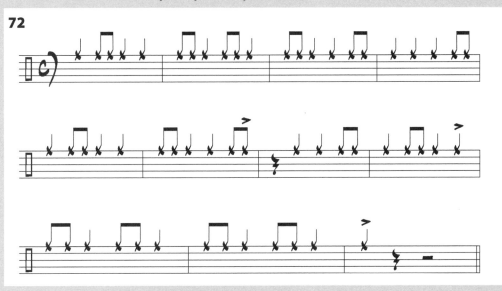

Ride Cymbal Sounds

Exercise 6 demonstrates how Bill uses the shoulder of the stick to play an accent on the cymbal without hitting it harder.

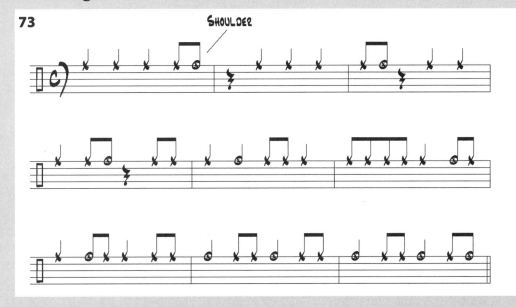

Left-Foot Independence

In Exercise 74, Bill demonstrates some left-foot hi-hat patterns while keeping time.

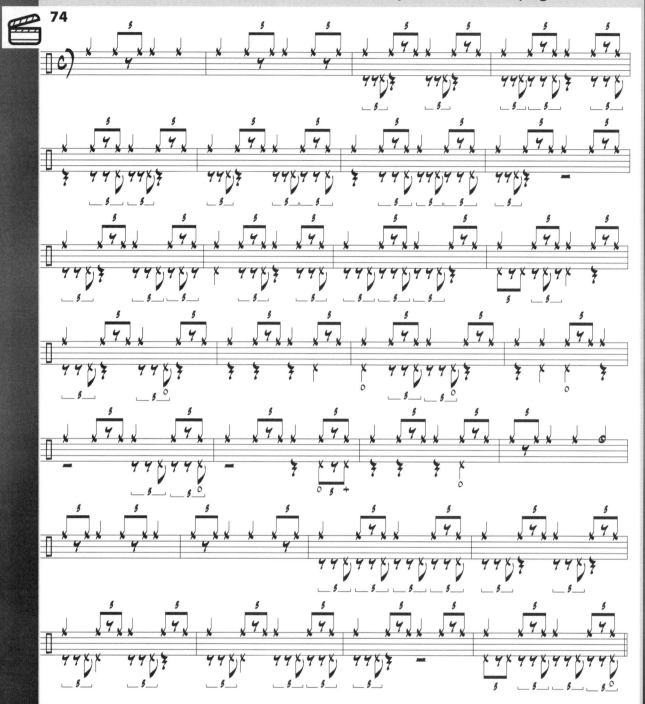

NOTES

NOTES